The Great Houses of San Francisco

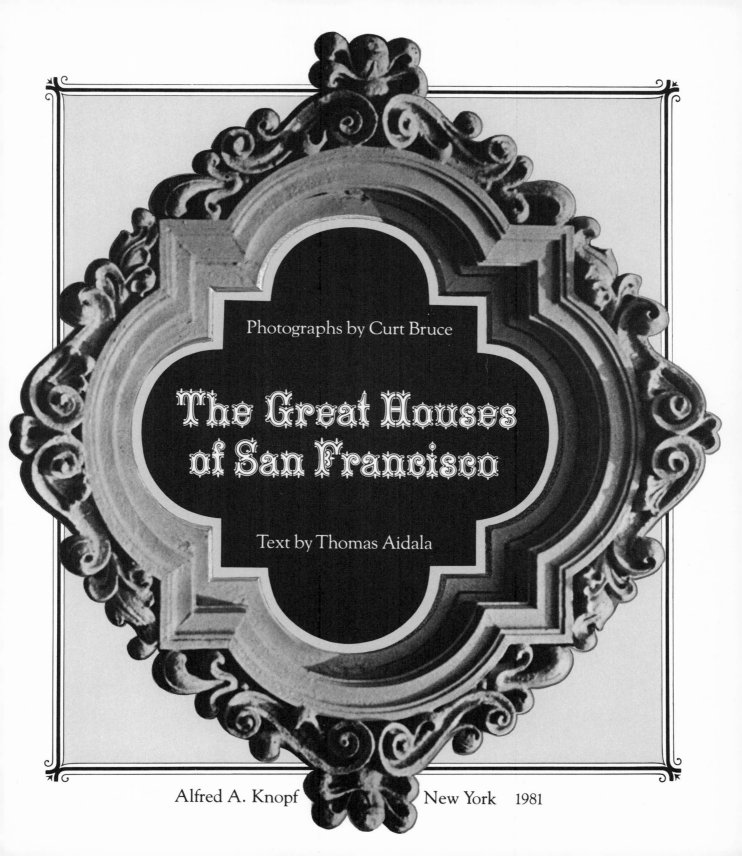

Photographs by Curt Bruce

The Great Houses of San Francisco

Text by Thomas Aidala

Alfred A. Knopf   New York   1981

THIS IS A BORZOI BOOK
PUBLISHED BY ALFRED A. KNOPF, INC.

Grateful acknowlegement is made to Harvard University Press
for permission to quote material from *Space, Time and Architecture,*
fifth edition, by Sigfried Gideon, published by Harvard University Press.
Copyright 1941, 1949, 1954, © 1962, 1967
by the President and Fellows of Harvard College.

The photographs on pages 5, 9, 10, 11, 12, 13, 14, 20, 39, and 40
are reproduced with permission from the collection of
The California Historical Society, San Francisco.

The photographs on pages 32, 33, 34, 35, and 36
are reproduced with permission from the collection of
The Bancroft Library, University of California at Berkeley.

ISBN 0-394-70773-7
Library of Congress Catalogue Card Number 73-7287

Manufactured in the United States of America

First Paperback Edition

To the unknown builders of
nineteenth-century San Francisco

Contents

Photographer's Note

Selecting the photographs that make up this book posed a complex problem, since San Francisco is a storehouse of architectural treasures. The most outstanding old building of most communities would be commonplace in San Francisco. The criterion for including a photograph was that the building be the best example of an important architectural trend, and that it have a unique atmosphere and character. This may explain why some famous buildings are not included.

Wandering through the city's streets, one is struck by the bits and pockets of old San Francisco scattered among the more recent notions of what a city should look like. As in Rome, the modern city has been built throughout and around the older complex. The living face of the city goes through its metamorphosis and, year by year, its past becomes harder to imagine, more dreamlike. This book is an attempt to freeze the flow of time, if only for a moment, and to experience that dream.

I would like to thank the following persons and organizations for their invaluable help and kind suggestions in realizing this collection: Mr. and Mrs. Stuart Adams—Bardelli's Restaurant—Frank Asch, Roger Baird, The Bancroft Library of the University of California at Berkeley, Bill Barich, Edward Bransten, Lee Burtis, Herb Caen,

The California Historical Society, Doug Clark, Richard Cole, Mr. and Mrs. Francis Ford Coppola, Lionel Craven, Peter Evans, Crescenzo Giasullo, Lorraine Hilton, Sherrye Jackson, Pennfield Jenson, Eleanor Jerricoff, Lynn Jerricoff, Harvey Jones, W. Dean Kirkpatrick, Linda Lieberman, Ernest R. Lilienthal, Don McCartney, The Norwegian Club of San Francisco, The Oakland Museum, Rai Okamoto, Bill Pearson, Henry Poirot, The San Francisco Public Library—Special Collections Division—Barry Silberstang, Harold I. Silverman, Mona Skager, Francis L. Stein, James Tyack, Ted Van Doren, Maria Vella, Walden House, Inc., and August Wegerman.

A brief note about my photographic technique might be of interest. All photographs except details were taken with a Nikon F camera equipped with the 35mm f/2.8 Perspective Correcting (PC) Nikkor lens. This lens incorporates an 11mm shift off center in its mount, thereby providing the equivalent of a rising or shifting front in a view camera. In practical terms, this PC lens permitted photographing the tops of buildings without the need to tilt the camera upward, thus preserving the vertical plane. Some of the detail pictures were made with a Nikon using a 135mm f/3.5 Auto-Nikkor, permitting isolation of significant detail.

The Great City

here is an indolence about the Bay Area and its surrounds that entices the stranger who first glimpses the round, tawny hills, their hump and hollow marked here and there by clumps of dark-green scrub oak and manzanita; it is a landscape that speaks to the senses. The land is close to water, yet hidden from it by hills. It is a dry area, and one realizes the proximity of bay and ocean only when fog or gulls settle far inland. On special days, atmosphere vanishes, and with the naked eye (depending on vantage point) one can see buildings thirty, forty miles away, with no intervening motion of air agitated by heat, moisture, or petrochemical fumes. It then becomes a landscape of exquisitely painful beauty: golden hills and blue-shaded valleys; stands of redwood, fir, laurel, oak, and manzanita; man's objects contained in the enormity of the land and a greater vault of light.

That is, on special days. On other days, it rains a lot or the fog rolls in and is not burned away by the late morning or afternoon sun. But even that is special. It is special when it rains days on end in winter and one begins to feel imprisoned by nature. It is special in any weather because the American dream stopped here on the Pacific shore. The nation ran out of land and had to stop running away from itself. It had no place left to run except inward. In San Francisco, the runners of the world who came to find gold created a life style and architecture not duplicated since.

In the middle of the nineteenth century, opportunistic gamblers, cut off from society—cut off, I imagine, from their own sense of proportion—suspended social decorum and notions of class and wagered on their own intuitions of an individual's worth in an incredibly fluid society. That society—San Francisco—was to become in the 1870s one in which maids, their fortunes built on silver speculations, entertained their former mistresses at six-course dinners and made small talk across the table with mercantile barons they once served. They would dine in rooms seductively rich in curlicue shadow and scroll work, the walls papered in perhaps six patterns, with stags and lions carved in wood, and occasionally nine-foot-long paintings of nude women; rooms rich enough to fill the mind when occasional silence prevailed across tables heaped with game and vegetables from Oregon, wines from France, and brandies from Chile.

That society was to develop its own rich aesthetic in a chancy time, a time when the gent in fawn-colored suede boots, silk hat atop hair "dressed and puffed and curled," would leave in his wake the scent of Macassar oil (and necessitate the invention of the antimacassar). That dude, as a writer for *The Gold City* described him, was "curiously compounded; he has a beaver on his head, a goat-ee on his chin, kids on his hands, calves on his legs; he casts sheep's eyes and is looked upon by his doe-ting duck as a deer at any price." That dandy would confront his ambition on the silver market. A busted mine, and he is back running a survey line, or heisting coaches, or dealing cards, or if luck, health, and looks run strong, pleasuring wealthy women. He might, if fortune nodded, run a careful string at a gaming table; if not, out of favor, fortune, fame, go back to work. A chancy time in a chancy place, where the mine would run out as sure as the fog, but the good goddess fortune ran her string and they made a sensual place—they made street after street of sensual places—in her honor.

Five days before the adoption of the Declaration of Independence on the eastern edge of the American continent, the first Mass on the western edge of that continent was celebrated by Father Francisco Palóu in a brush shelter on the shore of a lagoon off a great arm of the sea that was to become the site of San Francisco. Yet even that was not the beginning.

At the time of the founding in 1607 of Jamestown on the east coast, the Spaniards were already well seasoned by their New World experience. Leaving Manila, Spanish galleons sailing the great northern circle of the Pacific needed a port of call somewhere north of Mexico. Sebastian Rodríguez Cermeno was dispatched by a viceroy in Mexico to sail from Manila and find a sheltered place, with plenty of fresh water, where repair to vessels and men could be accomplished for the final leg of the journey to Acapulco, home port for the Philippine trade. The bay that Cermeno found in 1595, some twenty-five miles north of the present bay of San Francisco, is the one called Drake's Bay today, but Cermeno did what Drake himself had failed to do fifteen years earlier—he named it the Bay of San Francisco and got it on Spanish maps. The *San Augustín*, Cermeno's ship, was then driven ashore and totally wrecked. The crew, loyal to King, Country, and Cross (there was no great distinction among them) and not eager to choose wild California over Mexico, followed Cermeno down the coast in the ship's launch. Sailing between the Farallon Islands and across the mouth of the present San Francisco Bay in heavy fog, they failed to see it, just as the Portuguese Juan Rodríguez Cabrillo and the Englishman Drake had.

It was 170-odd years later, on November 2, 1769, that the great bay we now call San Francisco was discovered by Europeans. A band of priests and soldiers was sent north by land from San Diego by Viceroy Galvez to establish a mission honoring St. Francis at the Bay of San Francisco (Drake's Bay) to blunt Russian incursions south from Alaska. On the way, they were instructed to stop at Monterey Bay. Gaspar De Portola, the expedition's military leader, following notes that Vizcaino (another near-discoverer), had made on coastal features, took his group too far east on the coast, missed Monterey Bay entirely, and wandered to the north. Deciding he might be close, Portola sent his sergeant, José Ortega, to spy out a way to Point Reyes, which would identify the bay they were looking for. Impatiently awaiting the return of the sergeant, a group of hunters took to the hills to search for game. They topped a hill somewhere east of present-day Half Moon Bay and, to their surprise, looked down on an inland sea so vast that Father Crespi, accompanying the hunters, wrote later: "It is a harbor such that not only the navy of our most Catholic Majesty, but those of all Europe could take shelter in it." Ortega returned with confirmation of the claim—an arm of the sea prevented their approach to Point Reyes. In only one hundred years, that harbor indeed would be visited by more vessels than the navies of her Catholic Majesty or all Europe could claim.

On January 24, 1848, about 150 miles east of San Francisco, James Wilson Marshall, a carpenter in service to John A. Sutter (who managed a Mexican grant of land he called New Helvetia),

Yerba Buena (San Francisco) just before the Gold Rush (1849). Telegraph Hill is in the center.

observed in his millrace those metallic flakes, sparkling in the sun, that were to start the great gold rush. Ten days later, February 2, 1848, the Treaty of Guadalupe Hidalgo was signed, officially ending the war between Mexico and America, and only two years later, in 1850, California was admitted to the union. The irony of the United States collecting on the three hundred-year-old dues that the Spanish had paid in their not-so-serious attempts to bring Alta California firmly into the Spanish diadem was underscored by Marshall's discovery. For a short time after the discovery the *Californianos* had the streams and foothills to themselves. But when President James Knox Polk lifted the lid from a teapot conveyed by an official messenger, to marvel at three thousand dollars' worth of gold inside, the significance of the strike became clear. In December 1848, R. M. Patterson, the director of the mint in Philadelphia, accepted a deposit from Mr. David Carter of thirty-six thousand dollars' worth of gold.

He quickly recognized opportunity and filed an official report. Patterson's report, coupled with President Polk's message to Congress about his unexpected blessing, tipped the continent east to west and the rush was on.

Those rushing to seek gold in the foothills of the Sierra came not only from other parts of the United States but also from all parts of the world. San Francisco suddenly became a cosmopolitan city, passing from infancy to youth without intervening childhood: a salad of adventurers and foreigners whose language, style, and food were soon accommodated. In the early days of the rush, the stockpiling of supplies kept reasonable pace with the needs of fortune seekers. The Golden Gate—narrow outlet to the sea—became a funnel through which sailed an increasing number of vessels hauling immigrants and cargo. (The *Alta California* reported on August 17, 1852: "The ship Oscar from Havre [sic] brought about one-hundred daughters of La Belle France.") The newcomers must have been bewildered: on every side, tents and buildings just begun or only half completed; signs in all languages offering shovel and pick, flour and salt, eggs and pins; wagons churning great clouds of dust, hauling supplies from ships in the bay to those ramshackle structures.

Milling about on errands of commerce—mediating the polyglot influx—were New England Yankees of every cut, moving, mixing, and dealing with Mexicans and Chileans, Kanakas from the Hawaiian Islands, Samoans and Chinese. Dark under sombreros were the native Californians, supplying mules, food, and land to the mass of strangers and registering, however lightly, that this melee spelled the end of California for them. Amid the confusion, one activity and word was constant: speculation. The New York *Tribune* went for a dollar an issue; a room with no board at the Ward House cost $250. Cloth and pins, boots and banjos—everything was wanted, al-almost anything could be had at a price, and almost always there was someone to pay it. Along the regularly laid-out gridiron streets, houses were being built at the rate of fifteen to thirty a day. Hotels were flung up in all parts of the city, at first catering to simple needs, then, as the rush for gold turned into a wild dash for silver, becoming more luxuriously furnished in velvet and walnut, crystal and gilt, challenging known limits of height and then exceeding those limits by use of wood stick-built construction. The Ward House, the Graham House (brought entirely, stick and furniture, cup and pillow, from Baltimore), and later the Palace (*10–11*),* built in 1875,

*The italicized numbers in parentheses, here and throughout this essay, refer to the pages on which a building or particular architectural style under discussion is pictured.

successively established the par for luxury and style. Returning to San Francisco in the 1850s after just four months' absence, one would have seen a city transformed, extended, more populated. Some men came to work the fields, others to engage in commerce—and certain women came as well to engage in their special commerce with men. Albert Bernard de Russailh, a Frenchman who arrived in the '50s, noted in his diary: "There are also honest women in San Francisco, but not very many." Russailh describes a typical scene:

To sit with you near the bar or at a card table, a girl charges one ounce ($16 in gold) an evening. She had to do nothing save honor the table with her presence. This holds true of the girls selling cigars, when they sit with you. Remember, they only work in the gambling halls in the evening. They have their days to themselves and can receive all the clients who had no chance during the night. Of course, they often must buy dresses, and dresses are very expensive out here. For anything more you have to pay a fabulous amount. Nearly all these women at home [in France] were streetwalkers of the cheapest sort. But out here, for only a few minutes, they ask a hundred times as much as they were used to getting in Paris. A whole night costs from $200 to $400.

Gold and the race for it had caused the city to grow faster than almost any other before it, and the price of services corresponded to the physical growth: two to four hundred dollars a night for a prostitute, eighteen dollars for a dozen eggs, thirty-two dollars for a single visit with a doctor. It was not entirely the scarcity of supplies that caused prices to skyrocket; it was simply not worth the time to haggle over the cost of an article when hundreds of others were eager to pay anything for that same item in their hurry to get to the streams of gold. It is not surprising that quick wealth occasioned an enormous importation of goods. The Bay Area was not mobilized to provide for the kind of growth that transformed a small, nodding community of perhaps five hundred into a major metropolis in a little over twenty years.

San Francisco suddenly became a mercantile sponge absorbing cargo from the holds of thousands of ships. Crystal and chandeliers from Central Europe; glasses, door knobs, and silver from England; silks and porcelain from Japan; Bombay boxes; Hindu embroideries; wine and cloth from France; and women from all corners of the world found their way into the homes, hotels, whorehouses, and great brick buildings devoted to gambling, food, and luxury. The Bella Union, the Rendez-Vous, the Empire, and the Veranda were fitted out in bizarre excess by French companies syndicated across the Atlantic to profit from the natural resource the West had become. Anything that came in by ship was sold, and everything that *could* come in by ship *did* come. From the works of Hubert Howe Bancroft (writing of one of these gambling houses in the 1850s):

> In one, the ceiling, rich in fresco and gilt, was supported by glass pillars, pendant from which were great chandeliers. Around the walls were found large paintings of nude female figures, and mirrors extending from floor to ceiling. Entering at night from the unlighted dismal street into an immense room lighted with dazzling brilliance, and loud with the mingled sound of musical instruments, the clink of coin and glasses, and the hum of human voices, was like passing from the dark depths to celestial brightness.

From a wilderness, a void of sand dunes washed alternately by fog and rain and sun, from a brush chapel hard by a lagoon, the city had grown to accommodate the style of life and aesthetic will necessary for glass pillars and crystal chandeliers—a city peopled by voluntary exiles, dependent for mail and information on the steamers that arrived two or three times a month and on the daily stream of vessels carrying immigrants and supplies to provide links with a life left behind. It seemed as if the exiles, cut off from the center of American life and the culture of Europe, determined not to remain a backwater. They succeeded in creating an environment and social style, in fact a civic tone—one that not only mirrored but also attempted to rival the splendor of Europe, a tone that encompassed a special sociability and easy access to a style virtually nonexistent on the more settled east coast. It became a society rooted in change, and change was what made it tick. There was no vested interest in tradition; indeed, it could be argued that the only tradition there was, was to play the string out.

San Francisco has, from the beginning, captured the imagination of the country and the world as a place where our private myths might be made manifest and where eccentricity is not only grudgingly accepted but also expected. Writers have dwelled lovingly or cynically on its notable excesses—from vigilante escapades to fabulous balls, from fires to free lunches. The image of the city as party of the western world crystallized during the '60s and '70s: the fortunes of San Francisco ballooned out of sight with the discovery of the Comstock Lode in Nevada. The engines of growth, started by gold, fueled by silver, and run over the rails of the Central Pacific, were to run for four more decades.

Across the bay and up the Sacramento River in Sacramento, Charles Crocker had dealt in notions: thread, calico, corsets, gloves, and the like. Leland Stanford, a grocer, sold staples: beans, flour, candles, and canes. Collis Huntington and Mark Hopkins made grand profits from whatever they could push on miners at the jumping-off point to the gold country—shovels, picks, packs, and ammunition, whatever hard stuff was necessary up in the foothills. Spurred by the insistent dream of Theodore Judah, an engineer, that the railroad could and should be built, the four shopkeepers, who among them had anted up fifty thousand dollars, managed to bully, enjoin, entreat, and finally convince the city of San Francisco as well as the Central Pacific and Union Railroads (both creations, in fact, of the very building of the line itself) that it would be good business as well as a boost to manifest destiny to see the venture through. Ground was broken at Sacramento in 1863 for the building east to join the westward push initiated at the Missouri River by the Union Pacific. On May 10, 1869, at Promontory, Utah, San Francisco was finally joined to the rest of the nation by rail. Before a collection of politicians, financiers, and a group of Chinese (representative of the thousands of Chinese who had built the road in unspeakable bondage), the eastern half of the line was joined to the western half by Collis Huntington driving a golden spike into a tie of California laurel.

The railroad brought immediate economic benefits to San Francisco. Rather than the east becoming a market for what goods the city and California could produce, the opposite held true. Eastern goods flooded the coast and a minor balance of payments problem developed, but the problem was not one to give pause. The railroad was referred to as another of San Francisco's Aladdin's lamps. San Francisco had the foothills of the Sierra, as well as the Sierra itself, for treasury. Over the next two decades, the use and

importance of the railroad would grow to enormous proportions as the west was settled. The completion of the railroad almost coincided with the discovery of and speculation in silver, a speculation that made and broke many more fortunes than the discovery of gold had twenty years earlier.

The *Daily Morning Call* listed in August 1871 the 122 men who controlled 146 million dollars in the city. The article was titled "Mucho Dinero." Leland Stanford, ex-shopkeeper and now Governor and railroad king, had gone in nine years from trading beans to an estimated worth of ten million dollars. Ben Holiday of the Stage Coach Line teetered at a personal worth of over seven million. Michael Reese, in real estate and loans, was worth four million, as was James Phelan, dealer in liquor, real estate, and banking. The list went to many names but was not at all complete, and made no mention of the fortunes then building in San Francisco. But it did indicate the kind of money about. And when these parvenus (and the city itself was parvenu) decided to build, they built some rather remarkable structures, for the most part on what is now called Nob Hill.

James Ben Ali Haggin, the son of a Turkish mother and American father, was catholic in his successful financial enterprises. A lawyer by training, he operated with ease as owner of the Pacific Mail Wharf and Dock, in farming, mining, real estate, cattle raising, and horse breeding. He built the first mansion on Nob Hill, a modest sixty-room affair, some fifty feet high and ninety feet square, boasting three large conservatories. Two

Porter Ash Residence, address unknown. Burned, 1906.

years later, Leland Stanford gathered two million of his dollars and transformed them into home stables. The house had a Chinese room, its furniture a gift of the Chinese government; an Indian room; a Pompeian room; a purple-and-gold-velvet sitting room, and an art gallery with an oval velvet seat in the middle of the room. The center of the seat was filled with plants whose branches supported mechanical birds that, at the touch of a button, would serenade one with bird song.

Banker W. C. Ralston, owner and builder of the Palace Hotel *(10–11)*, was worth only a million and a half dollars in the *Call* listing; he bought, remodeled, and expanded a château one Count Cipriani had built in 1854 in a place called Canada de Diablo (now Belmont), south of San Francisco on the peninsula. All the partitions of Ralston's house were designed to slide into the walls or up into the ceilings in order that salons of various sizes could be fashioned for dinners and receptions. The doors were crystal panels (mytho-

Palace Hotel. Burned, 1906.

logical designs were chased into the crystal) with silver knobs; a silver balustrade edged the balconies overlooking a central skylighted inner court that led to the ballroom, whose walls, floor to ceiling, were covered with mirrors from Versailles. Ralston had installed an air cooling system, his own gas works, an elaborate gate that was mechanically raised whenever a coach hit a certain plank in the road, and a system of mirrors around the main staircase to capture its users at quite surprising angles. Crocker spent $2,300,000 on his city-block-sized home (12–13), only to be outdone by Mark Hopkins, who dumped three million into his (14). Even the stables of these houses, it was said, had crystal chandeliers. The rosewood stalls with silver trappings had mosaic floors covered with rugs from Brussels.

People in that time and place were deep into money and material goods, not just for conspicuous reasons, it seems, but because they knew it was all transitory anyway. They attempted to delight every one of their senses. Bronze peacocks with real peacock feathers, cornices of Roman, Greek, and Gothic influences; silk tassels; painted leather and cloisonnéd anything; silver and satin chairs; Chinese screens; deer head ornaments;

The Grand Court, Palace Hotel. Burned, 1906.

Charles Crocker Mansion, architect's elevation.

rosewood chamber sets; highboys of ebony; Turkish whatnots — think of it, and what you think of and more furnished these houses. At a dinner at the home of Leland Stanford, given for a circle of select friends, the waiter placed a large silver platter on the table. Stanford then rose and lifted the cover off the platter to introduce his son of a few weeks lying on a bed of blossoms. Baby, blossoms, and platter were carried around the table and shown to applauding guests.

Such was the age. Such nerve or verve or uninhibited involvement with the pleasure of life and display of it would be unthinkable today. We have, for the most part, been lacquered over by time and generations of manner, style, structure,

and history in our hunt after a respectably refined national image.

In 1859, Old Pancake Comstock, boarding with Eilley Orrum in her home at Gold Gulch, Nevada, would spend many a night (if legend lies in truth) huddled about Eilley's table with other prospectors as Mrs. Orrum urged her boarders north to Mount Davidson with visions pried from a crystal ball. Sometime later that year, when old Pancake was foraging about a mountain ravine, prying and picking at rock, he found gold quartz with a strange ore in it. At Nevada City, Pancake learned

Charles Crocker Mansion, California Street between Mason Street and Taylor Street. Burned, 1906.

from the assayer that the ore was silver, and that it yielded in volume value twice as much as gold. That silver did trickle into San Francisco during the '60s and did not make much of a wave in the sea of concern with gold is not surprising. The amount was small, the mining difficult and expensive. The lodes were just not worth the time, energy, or money. In 1872, however, the aorta of the Comstock mine was severed and silver spurted about over the now twice-blessed San Francisco; for every Stanford, Hopkins, or Huntington, there were scores more who would make it on a somewhat more human scale.

The development of a silver mine is an expensive operation compared with the coaxing of gold from soil by water. A man working for gold could make a decent enough poke with only shovel, pick, and a pan, playing by a stream. But silver was something else. Silver is widely distributed around the globe, but the total amount present compared to other ores is minuscule. There are only two parts of silver available for every ten million parts of iron; those two parts are found deep in mountains, and chasing the gold quartz that imprisons the silver is mean, hard-rock mining. Chasing required that deep shafts or long tunnels or both had to be sunk and dug, and it was not work for the entrepreneur and partner to engage in by hand, for by hand it was one man holding an iron drill and another pound-

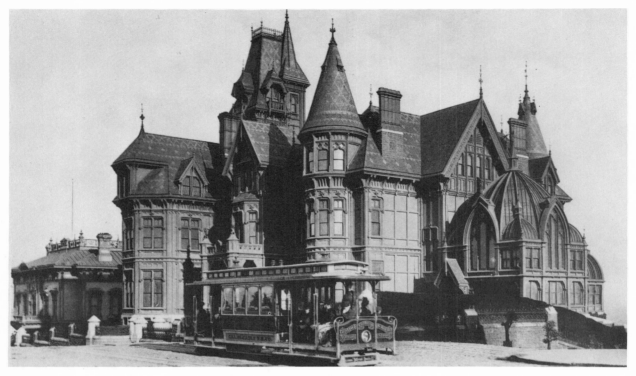

Mark Hopkins Mansion, California Street and Mason Street.   Burned, 1906.   Present site of Mark Hopkins Hotel.

ing with a ten-pound sledge hammer. Perhaps in an hour, perhaps in two, a hole in the granite two or three inches in diameter and two or three feet deep would be managed. Blasting powder would be poured in, and the charge would be fused, rammed with sand, and set. The explosion might result in a half yard of stubborn quartz—if one were lucky. In short, by any simple means, nudging silver from its nesting place was an arduous task, which, in most cases, yielded small return for the effort expended. Silver miners needed expensive machinery to reach the ore, huge stamping mills to pulverize the ore to powder, water to render it to slurry paste, and elaborate

refining systems to free the silver from the paste. The process needed to be made subject to large-scale industrialization: an industrialization whose appetite and feeding could only be satisfied by vast amounts of money.

That money was found at the Stock Exchange in San Francisco. Mines or false mines were discovered, and all were listed equally with the Exchange. The whole population, it seemed, played that market: housewives, whores, dentists, ministers, Chinese laborers, Italian farmers, French waiters, millionaires, servant girls, and clerks. Paper was floated like confetti on New Year's Eve, swindles were common, but the mines needed money and the returns were fantastic if you got out in time. California Mine stock went from $90 a share to $790; Consolidated Virginia was listed at $150 and went to $710. The names were as rich and fanciful as the time: Challar Potasi, Yellow Jacket, Ophir, and Savage. Ophir, worth almost nothing when listed, would sell in a year at $4,000 a foot. San Francisco never felt the slightest tremor of the eastern economic earthquake of the depression of the 1870s; the fortune of the city rose consistently and the population with it. When gold was discovered the city had a population of about 500 people; ten years later that number was 56,000, and it would go to 235,000 by 1880. Such growth coupled with steady wealth surely does something to the communal psyche.

When the nineteenth century began, wooden construction of dwellings had not been significantly altered for many centuries. Skilled and proficient laborers, schooled in expensive and tedious traditions, pegged, mortised, and tenoned away, heaving oversized wooden members, erecting structurally overdesigned buildings, operating within a technological process completely out of step with the demands of the growing frontier. "If it had not been for the knowledge of the balloon frame, Chicago and San Francisco could never have arisen as they did, from little villages to great cities in a single year," wrote Solon Robinson in the New York *Tribune* in January 1855. One year was perhaps a bit hyperbolic even for San Francisco, but Mr. Robinson was making a point. The invention of the balloon frame, a system of construction (called "stick-built") held together by nails and dependent upon sawmill machinery, was the only system that could meet the demands of the growing frontier.

In 1777, in Cumberland, Rhode Island, Jeremiah Wilkinson had devised the first recorded process of cutting nails from cold metal rods. It was a primitive process that led to a dead end, but out of the 120 patents issued during the next fifty years for nail-cutting machines based on Wilkinson's design, the variation patented by Ezekial Reed in 1786 led to modern nail-making. Cut nails eventually gave way to wire nails (more readily produced), and an industry was ready to deliver the estimated sixty-five thousand nails necessary for the building of a five-room balloon frame (stick-built) house. Previously the home builder had been a skilled carpenter who, as an apprentice, had learned to manipulate wood by shaping, cutting, pegging, and grooving. The balloon frame did away with the need for the skilled carpenter; unskilled laborers could and did erect thousands of stick-built houses. G. E. Woodward, in *Woodward's Country Homes* (1865) wrote: "A man and boy can now attain the same results with ease, that twenty men could on an old fashioned frame . . . the principle of Balloon Framing is the true one for strength as well as for economy. If a mechanic is employed, the Balloon Frame can be put up for forty percent less money than with the mortice and tenon frame." So, at the time when it was needed, a new method of building was invented. It is clear that the development of a fast, economical, uncomplicated, and sound system of construction accelerated the speed of settlement—and that, in turn, the speed of settlement necessitated better, faster, cheaper, and easier methods of building. No other place had quite the same need for speed or potential to provide the raw materials as did the Pacific coast. Douglas fir and redwood, from as far north as Oregon and as far south as Point Conception, grew in staggering abundance. Both woods are soft and easy to cut, yet both are also extremely strong, with clear, open grains, not given to splintering or splitting when nails are driven through them.

Technique and technology were available to help shape the architecture and furniture of the period to San Francisco's collective aesthetic urge, an exaggerated expression of an eclectic time in England as well as in the northeastern part of the United States. The mechanical router, the gang jig saw, and the iron steam press made it possible to bend, carve, shape, and stamp wood inexpensively into any desired form. They worked wood as we today work plastic. What happened, baldly stated, was that it all came together—technology, history, a growing middle class, and an extremely confident city far from the economic crisis of the 1870s back east.

During the latter half of the nineteenth century in San Francisco, the fortunes of the city were a product of what was taken from the mines. The city grew to become the economic, social, and cultural capital of the west. It mattered little if you mined in Utah or raised cattle in Colorado, you dropped your money eventually in San Francisco. As a major city, San Francisco needed all of the attendant services to supply its own needs as well as provide for an expanding and settling western frontier. A mercantile and manu-facturing base was immediately begun and expanded, employing tens of thousands in recently built wood or brick factories producing everything from shovels to shirts. The economic pulse quickened as trade, commerce, and industry grew at the same remarkable rate with which riches were extracted from the earth. The elaborate profits from mining made it all hum and buzz. Mining created the employment opportunities in other areas that allowed for the growth of an increasingly more comfortable middle class—and the need to house it.

The early houses—built in the '50s and in the '60s (17–18)—were for the most part small, box-like structures, as unassuming as the dented desires of those who did not float on the golden bubble of their ambition but had to become the providers of services, who had to join those others who just came for the chance to do what they did best in a place where perhaps there was money to pay them for their skills: the plumbers, bakers, dentists, carpenters. Those single-story houses were usually built a half story up from the ground. A direct flight of stairs from the sidewalk terminated at a door in the middle of the façade, flanked by two small windows. The façade was a typical frontier false front rising above the roof and trimmed with some cornice work (76), elaborating the hint of chic hunted after by the not-so-affluent persons within. The two-story houses were just as simple but not quite as unassuming, suggesting the extra money needed to purchase or build that extra floor. The windows were simply popped out from the plane of the façade, hinting at the extravaganzas of bay windows to come. They were all built of wood and went on in serried ranks, wall to wall, filling the ubiquitous twenty-five-foot-wide lot, up and down hill, and

963 14th Street.

painted in the popular colors of the time: from pale almost-yellow to dark yellow, almost brown.

But not all residences built in the '60s were unassuming and without gift of style. Perhaps the finest remaining example of this period was the three-storied Casebolt house, built in 1865–6 *(19)*. Intended by Henry Casebolt to house his wife and eleven children, it is almost a textbook of the style. Built of wood to simulate rusticated stone, all its elements are disposed symmetrically about a center entrance and porch. Quoins, arched windows, pediments, elaborate bracketed cornices, and balustrades are all perfectly preserved today. The only change from the original

is that the white outside was flecked with black paint to more nearly simulate stone. The formalism of the house extended out to the garden as well, with its pairing of cypresses and palms reinforcing the symmetry of the approach. The Casebolt house was almost the epitome of the silver period; it also came virtually at the end of that period.

The growth of San Francisco meant movement west—what little west was left. The city was founded on the eastern side of the peninsula, facing the sun and protected from the chilling fog by a pair of hills up the center of the northern end of the peninsula—Nob Hill and Russian Hill. It

2121–2123 Bush Street.

Casebolt House. 2727 Pierce Street.

grew the only way it could, given the thrust of the mythic imperatives of the nation and those who came: westward beyond those hills toward the ocean, claiming mile after mile of sand dunes. The "Western Addition" *(21, 81)*, as it was called, housed the growing middle class, the comfortable working class.

During the '80s and '90s, the city did not experience the overwhelming flood of profits from gold and silver that had been the norm in the previous decades. It continued, though, to experience a steady growth now made more stable by a balancing of the economic base. The Western Addition continued to grow, as did the Mission District (south of Market Street, around Mission Dolores), comfortably housing the prospering shopkeepers who lived above their stores, the doctors, importers, and underwriters, the solid burghers. Behind the imposing fronts of bay windows, in rooms stuffed with all manner of object and plant, a life went on away from the flash and glitter of those in thrall of wealth, whose instincts led to play with fortune downtown in the stock market, or with pleasure among the cribs in the Barbary Coast or the alleys of Chinatown, or with both fortune and pleasure in the gaming halls

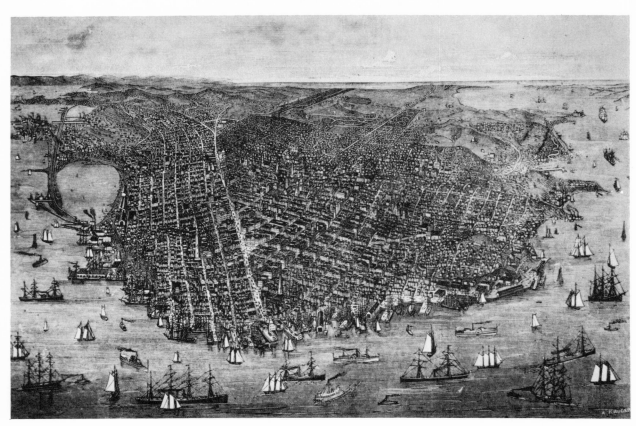

San Francisco, circa 1885.

1213–1215 Scott Street.

still extant. Congeries of the most incredibly bizarre and whimsically extravagant private residences were constructed throughout the Western Addition. Turkish cupolas (22) and Italianate porticoes (23) hung from Gothic buildings. Travelers east to New York, Boston, Philadelphia, and Washington, as well as to Paris and London, returned with architectural notions—and, in a few cases, with architects. Mostly, these buildings came to pass not by blueprint, but by whim: carpenters would add the exotic, the profane, the sublime purely on impulse (148–9). Some of the most attractive house fronts were not even the product of a carpenter's imagination—a good number of façades came prefab, shipped in crates from the east. It didn't matter if the front extended six or more feet above the natural roof line of the house (24); it didn't matter if, viewed

4040 17th Street.

from the side, a proud and artful façade seemed quite literally to be glued to an otherwise ordinary house *(25)*. In the popular mind of the late 1800s, it all worked. The Vedanta Society Temple *(170–3)*, designed by Joseph A. Leonard, successfully demonstrates a basic belief of the Hindu religion: that all religions are authentic and wise instru-

ments for finding the way. Practically all of the styles having currency at the time are displayed: Queen Anne, Moorish columns, Mogul arches, a crenelated tower, and bay windows.

That some of the buildings did, indeed, have architects is today almost incidental; when the old city hall was destroyed in the fire and quake of

819 Eddy Street.

2661–2673 Clay Street.

1906, building records were destroyed as well. The houses of the silver and early postsilver era — the houses that line the streets of the Western Addition — are anonymous entities. They are not, considered today, the fruit of a school, a style, a particular imagination; they are the offspring of a way of life.

Hence, Victorian architecture as we have come to call it is a misnomer, especially in San Francisco, since this term identifies a variety of styles and competing aesthetic pressures by placing them within the historical context of the nineteenth century and referring that century to the rule of Victoria in England. In England was to be seen for the first time the architectural influence of two men, one English and the other French, and the influence stretched to — and became stretched in — San Francisco.

John Ruskin's life nearly spanned the century: he was born in 1819 and died in 1900, and was well known as an author, art critic, and social reformer. The Frenchman was Viollet-le-Duc, a ferret of the twelfth and thirteenth centuries and archeologist of Gothic architecture. In 1851, Ruskin published the results of a trip to Italy, where he had pondered Italian Gothic architecture. *Stones of Venice* was available the same year in the United States and its impact was immediate. Probably the first result of Ruskin's book was a reawakening to the potentials of polychrome, both of materials and paint, and an infatuation with medieval proportion and detail, especially as seen in works of northern Italy. Three years later, in 1854, Viollet-le-Duc published the first of ten volumes that were to take him until 1868 to complete. The work, entitled the *Dictionnaire Raisonné de l'Architecture,* was a heroic attempt to create a calculus of architecture based on his ruminations on the Gothic period. It was a plea for moral exactitude and functional directness, as well as for that most desired marriage of hand and eye, form and content.

These scholarly influences, dwelling as they did on the Gothic, were too much of a downpour on the intellectual aridity of the architectural landscape of western Europe in the 1850s. Archi-

tects seized on this coherent body of architectural theory (the only such body of theory in almost one hundred years) and at once began to elaborate on it. By the middle of the 1860s, England saw the development of a style which became known as Modern English Gothic—in the words of one contemporary critic—"a most sincere and simple style."

With the clangor of Ruskin's and Viollet-le-Duc's honest Gothic admonitions ringing in his head, Sir Charles L. Eastlake published in 1868,

2247 Turk Street.

both in America and England, *Hints on House-hold Taste*; the book soon disabused America of its notion of form as expression of the content of life style, and instead opened up vistas of architecture-as-fruit-salad. Eastlake's work treated of furniture mostly, and of the stern moral value of a construction system based on joined medieval woodworking details—massive pieces of furniture held together by pegs alone. In America that style became known as the Eastlake style, one which banished pad and curve to a purgatory reserved for the impure. This notion was indeed at odds with commercial trade furniture of the time, which was sensibly padded and curved to receive the body in comfortable embrace. It was theory versus comfort. In America, comfort had prevailed (especially in San Francisco), but inroads were made by Eastlake. Wood was honestly stained and no longer French-lacquered. Eastlake's pieces and the more popular trade furniture were both substantially different from the delicate French Rococo, still influential in England, and the American Shaker style, delicate and light enough to support the admiring glance of a 260-pound plutocrat, but surely not his trust. The desire for clarity confused some architects but fascinated and converted others to the Neo-Gothic imperatives of Ruskin and Viollet-le-Duc: structural expression, a slenderness of structured members, each doing its job and no more; the reduction of non-essential carving and decoration to a gathering of decoration coincidental with the gathering of structural stresses, real or imagined; glazing the infill between structural elements as much as reason prevailed or stability allowed; and the use of color, both inside and out.

What allowed for the creation of a style of residential architecture out of the whole cloth for the first time in history were the change in family structure and the enormously increased wealth generated by the refinements of the industrial revolution. The social and physical mobility effected by the opportunities to wealth and the industrial revolution's readiness to produce the machines to make mass housing possible and profitable were at the root of this change. Opportunity coupled with need birthed desire. When the opportunity came from streams of gold and veins of silver, desire was substantial at birth.

Victorian Gothic, Italianate, and to a smaller extent the Turkish, Egyptian, and other less important romantic styles arrived on the east and west coasts almost simultaneously. The climate of thought and experience was receptive to the possibilities that these styles offered—possibilities primarily of the asymmetrical open plan (27), reflecting a heightened awareness of man's interdependence with nature, whose colors, textures, and lines were beginning to be duplicated in scrollwork, sewing, and stained-glass windows. The asymmetrical plan freed living patterns from the rigid symmetry of Colonial New England and Southern plantation residential architecture: an architecture that disposed parts about a central axis both in plan and evaluation. The new freedom allowed for towers, loggias, balconies, interior rooms of all shapes to be arranged ingeniously and dynamically, suiting topography, views, and owners' whims. The rejection of the symmetrical represented perhaps the first architectural revolution in the United States. Although the new styles were grounded in the past, they were by no means mere revivals or even survivors of earlier styles; they represented instead an awareness and creative use of older principles to suit an emerging life style in an emerging place.

1333, 1335 Hayes Street.

443 Fair Oaks Street.

From the '60s through the '80s, reflecting a growing affluence and stability, the houses of the middle class became more and more elaborate and Italianate. Italian Gothic *(28)*, with its low-pitched, bracketed roofs, loggias, and boxlike form, had become the pervasive stylistic fuel driving architecture on both coasts. The homes, spreading out block on block in the Western Addition, and pushing the dunes farther from downtown, became increasingly crystalline as the solid façades began to dissolve before a preoccupation with glass, light, and the minimalization of apparent structure. The bay window now ran from street to roof *(below)*, dominating the houses and making of entire street fronts a faceted wall of glass and color, rich in chiaroscuro and reflection. The architecture was (and remains) one that worked to engage and delight the eye at all levels of scale, from groupings of two or three blocks as one looked down the street, to the individual details surrounding a window or announcing an entrance *(118–19)*. These building façades were completely integrated and at ease with themselves. The details—scrolls, fretwork, fans, cut and beveled glass, stringcourses—were all conceived to capture the eye and captivate the mind with no-

605–611 Haight Street.

2415, 2417 Franklin Street.

tions of craft as well as with the sensuousness of the play of light over form. Towers and turrets with Turkish cupolas and mansard roofs were freely added to the basic Italianate building block, as balusters, dentils, lion heads, and rosettes lovingly and playfully crawled over the façades *(left, below, 31, 184)*.

2415, 2417 Franklin Street.

724 Shrader Street.

Dwelling exclusively on the exteriors of these houses suggests that care was expended only in an attempt to seduce or impress the viewer without. Not so. As the passerby had eventually to turn into one of these homes, so too did that same reach for baroque excess curl over and around doorjambs and on through the front door into the reception hall *(below)*. The halls were announcements of the personal wealth of the occupants and were always more splendid than the rest of the rooms. Whether the family was rich, not so rich, comfortable, or just making it could be read by the size, decoration, and furnishings that greeted the visitor upon entering. For the most part, once

Interior, circa 1890.

beyond the reception hall the sense of visual engagement that occurred outside occurred inside with the furnishings. Usually upon entering a modest home one would be at the end of a corridor leading directly to back rooms, kitchen, and pantry. Off right and left would be two doors to study and parlor (*above*) and immediately beyond the parlor door would be a flight of stairs half as wide as the corridor leading to upper floors. A more costly home would have a spacious, impos-

ing hall sometimes two stories in height, paneled in rich mahogany, zebrawood, walnut, or the ever-present redwood stained purple-brown and varnished to violin-back sheen. If not to ceiling, the paneling went to chair-rail height, and above the wainscot the walls were covered in deep-green cloth or paper rich in texture and design.

Inhabiting these entries were several pieces of furniture essential to the vigorous etiquette of the day. A large, elaborately carved stand for hats,

Interior, circa 1890.

coats, canes, and umbrellas would stand against the wall, often built integrally as part of the house. The more complex examples combined a bench for sitting while waiting favor. Two arms served as repositories for umbrellas or silver-knobbed walking sticks; above the bench was a mirror, small oval to larger than full-figure height. On either side of the mirror were well-turned pegs or hooks to hold cloaks and beaver hats. Either combined with the stand or on a separate table, depending on the size of the hall, was to be found a salver to receive the visitor's calling card. Beyond the hall, the rooms of the larger houses were grouped into three parts with some overlap: the private suite consisting of bedrooms, family room, library or study, morning room, kitchen, and pantry. Reception rooms included dining room, reception hall, or drawing room, at times morning room and study, and, if fortune grinned upon the family, a large ballroom usually upstairs under the roof—or on the ground floor if fortune's grin became hysterical. The third component was the servants' quarters, which again, depending on wealth, could be either a suite or a room.

With the increasing affluence of the silver years owners and builders often indulged their whims by including within the house rooms of a very specific purpose. Smoking rooms were for men to retire to, someplace to loosen a vest and puff away on a fine fat cigar after dinner or during a reception. The smoking room was necessary since smoking in the rest of the house, at least on formal occasions, was not viewed with ease. As the century drew to a close and it became acceptable to trail clouds of fine Havana wherever, this room continued to be included (I suspect simply because it was not considered proper for women to enter it). It became, along with the billiard room, the domain principally of men, while women staked out the morning room (*below*) and drawing room during the day.

By whatever strange alchemy, the urge for and

Interior, circa 1890.

love of green plants within the house reached almost hallucinatory proportions. Plants were everywhere, stuffed in corners, hanging from ceilings, and perched on newel posts. If money allowed, you could almost always find a conservatory, a wonderful glass room, just off the drawing room on the first floor, filled with plants growing around an artificial pond fed by trickling water, which often contained goldfish and occasionally frogs. These rooms came in all sizes, from Huntington's enormous conservatory (which could have served a small city as botanical garden) to those of less heroic circumstance: a window on a stair landing would contain a glass box and there plants would grow modestly—unless that window was an incredibly explosive stained-glass fantasy produced by one of the many art glass studios that dotted the city.

It was the stained-glass windows (*opposite; see also color photographs following page 84*) and the Oriental and Middle Eastern rugs that provided the pure brilliant colors in a color scheme

Circa 1890.

that, aside from the plants, went to deep moody shades. The popularity of commercial stained-glass windows entered in the early 1900s as a concomitant of Art Nouveau—an import from France and Belgium. Though Art Nouveau never made an enormous impact on the architecture of the time, it did, about 1905, begin to shape hardware, furniture, and bric-a-brac, at least in those urban centers that could afford the luxury of indulging avant-garde desires. Following Tiffany's ventures and the popularity of the pre-Raphaelites, those organically sinuous shapes and some-what sensuously decadent depictions of fish, outrageous fowl, flowers, hybrid trees, and curious geometrics began to appear in glass windows, doors, roundels, and free-standing screens, always illuminating a consciously designed pool of gloom with brilliant-colored, light-delineated, highly stylized plant and animal forms.

Toward the end of the nineteenth century, H. P. Berlage, a Dutch architect of major influence on

841 Fulton Street.

the modern movement, wrote, "Our parents and grandparents as well as ourselves have lived and still live in surroundings more hideous than any known before . . . lying is the rule, truth the exception." To the modern generation of architects schooled on the Bauhaus and the ethic of efficiency, it was difficult indeed to look on these buildings when initially confronted with them and see anything but the objects of the tasteless, concerned only with display and conspicuous consumption. These are notions of a politically motivated architectural education, an education concerned primarily with consolidating the fruits of an artistic revolution which saw the plastic experience as total, as well as universally applicable.

Modern architects were unable to *see* these buildings, trained as we were in a stylistic ambience that viewed architecture as a universal, abstract, and unrelenting art: an art which is dependent for its authenticity not on the joy produced, but on technical theories of structural efficiencies, and aesthetic theories of moral purity and universality. The generation and acceptance of these views in the first half of this century paralleled the rise of other political theories of moral purity and universality (which came to be known as totalitarianism), as well as notions of ill-defined social function or utility, and ignored the potential impact of local life style upon architecture and politics. Architectural style in the mainstream of our century be-

The third Cliff House. Near Sutro Baths on the Great Highway. Burned, 1907.

came exclusionary and reductive in its quest for universality, rather than inclusionary and additive, as these buildings are. Since carving a stick, we believed, did not make it any more able to support a table or a roof, it therefore reeked of moral decadence. As a result of this cramped ideology, eclecticism became pariah, and "Victorian" architecture, viewed through the lens of an aggressively inhibited and basically Protestant morality, was castigated, attacked, and vilified; the mind and the body separated, and experience became idea.

But living with these stick-built marvels over the years, looking at them in all qualities of light, becoming dimly aware of the time in which they were produced, we slowly learned that rather than being issue of smothered creativity, they were the results of a truly explosive outburst of creative energy. Energy that was able to translate

Sutro Baths. Sutro Heights. Demolished.

into wood and brick and stone an existential optimism, by using all available ideas and technologies in a way they had never been used before to create a new and authentic architecture that spoke with its own tongue—this was what built San Francisco.

The buildings were eclectic because the times were as eclectic as the inhabitants of the city. It was inevitable that the architecture would reflect that quick, crazy mixture, and if among them there are some buildings that are exquisitely ugly and excessively bizarre, there are others that are perfectly proportioned and exquisitely beautiful. Perhaps the ease with which contradictory and disparate styles were accepted and willingly placed side by side had as much to do with the disparate and contradictory times of the country as a whole as with the ethnic and existential diversity of San Francisco.

It was a period of seemingly introspective, yet violently aggressive musing among artists and intellectuals on the nature of the United States: democracy, the condition of the citizen, the state of its art, the nature of its economy, and the development of a self-image not made in the mold of Europe. It was a period of contradictory themes and issues that divided the country politically, socially, and philosophically and extended the dialogue over these issues back and forth across the continent. The country was witnessing intense urban growth on the one hand and the growth of an agrarian-born population on the other. Industrialization vied with handcraft methods of production that took advantage of an ever-increasing immigration from Europe and the resultant pool of craftsmen. It was a time that saw almost every one of the crafts necessary to the building industry organize and establish unions. Carpenters, elec-

tricians, plumbers, brick and stone masons, painters, and elevator workers were all organized within the context and fervor of the labor movement. It was a time of great economic concentrations, public outcry against such concentrations, and legislative responses to the outcry for control of the growth and power of the great combines. The urges of the men who ran the trusts and monopolies were essentially imperial, and it is not surprising that their aesthetic was also generally imperial. It is extremely difficult to build a modest, self-effacing house for a million dollars or more; it was not surprising, therefore, that the great stone palaces of this period were, in their own way, as incredibly powerful as the wealthy families who lived in them.

The Frick house, in New York, designed by Hastings of the office of McKim, Mead and White, the Morgan mansion, built by the same office in the same city, and the Flood mansion in San Francisco, built in 1885 of imported Connecticut sandstone and designed by Augustus Laver, were beautiful examples of revival and derivative architecture, whose proportions and combinations of formal elements transcended origins and became significant works able to stand or fall on their own merits. These palazzi were subjected to the pitiless criticism of social reformers of the time who attacked the buildings and their owners as being overly opulent, even immoral. Henry Demerest Lloyd said of the owners that they were "without restraint of culture, experience, the pride, or even the inherited caution of class or rank." They were viewed as one-generational men. (But then, even today the romantic notion that joins virtue and poverty still holds among many social observers and social engineers.)

In their revivalist zeal, the architects who dealt

Main Post Office. 7th Street and Mission Street.

with these men and who built the large homes and libraries, hotels, and other civic buildings created an architecture which became a masterful mix of Renaissance, baroque, French classical, Gothic, and whatever else was handy. While some were successfully tossing styles, others were tossing in rage. A national debate within the architectural profession divided the east (New York) from the west (Chicago) and saw Root, Jenney, Holabird, Sullivan, and the young Wright pitted against the solidified establishment of McKim, Mead, White, Cram, Hunt, and Hastings of New York. The dialogue or debate was mainly one way—west to east, the easterners being at all odds too comfortable to engage the notions of cow-country ideologues.

The Chicago bunch, comfortable themselves in the mainstream of populism and in thrall to Walt

Main Post Office.   7th Street and Mission Street.

Whitman, whose "Democratic Vistas" conjured up visions of a uniquely American civilization, saw the need, or felt the need, for a demandingly modern, non-historically based, quintessentially American architecture; an architecture that owed nothing to the past, but one that constantly mirrored the constantly changing historical, technological, social, and evolutionary conditions of the country. The Chicago radicals believed, as Whitman did, that there is an unavoidable connection between democracy and the primacy of the individual, and they made the leap to the conclusion that the architecture of a democracy is an architecture of unique buildings shaped by the pressures of the building program and of changing social and economic conditions. The inevitability of the form of all systems at a point in time had been made eminently clear by Darwin and, in his own small way, by Gottfried Semper, a German architect and theoretician having much currency in Chicago then. Herr Semper wrote, "Style is the conformity of an art object with the circumstance of its origin and the conditions and circumstances of its development"—a statement that could, if vigorously applied, justify all manner of entrepreneurial aesthetics. That American architecture derived its form from Europe did not disturb too large a segment of the profession. That the revolutionaries read dark conspiracies in each French Renaissance or Italian baroque façade was to be expected; revolutionaries see conspiracy everywhere.

The Italianate style of the 1860s was followed in popularity by the French influence of the Second Empire *(118-19)*. An era of new and easy wealth looking for majestic identity seemed to have found it in the opulent furnishings of the French court. Travelers abroad, influenced by the social life of Napoleon III and his wife, Eugénie, and the physical surround of that sociability, returned with desires for, and architects schooled in, oval *(45)* and segmental arch windows, mansard roofs *(46)*, coupled columns, and broken pediments. It was not long after 1880 that these elements began to appear in San Francisco. The general architectural result of this influence was a cooler, disdainful try at elegance and a return to symmetry while maintaining the busy involvement with detail. As a "pure" style it did not meet with much success in the city, though bits and pieces were used widely, mainly the mansard roofs and oval windows. When an attempt at the French was made, it was usually done by reproducing existing buildings, such as the exact replica of Le Petit Trianon at Versailles built for Marcus Koshland in 1902. (In fact, there are at least four reproductions and adaptations of that building along the peninsula.) Paul Phillippe Cret wrote, "Nobody imposed French architecture on the United States. It was of their own free will that hundreds of Americans went to Paris and that thousands more took their inspiration from the ideas they brought back. Were all these men fools? What were they looking for in France? . . . It was composition and design."

The generations of architects who followed Louis Sullivan and Frank Lloyd Wright often carried ideas of those two to unsuspected ends— as when they attempted to demonstrate that the Columbian Exposition in Chicago of 1893 sounded the death knell to American architecture for the next fifty years. It was the kind of rhetoric that fit the heroic myths upon which the new

2055-59 Powell Street.

3341 Washington Street.

architects were schooled. Anything that did not spring from either Chicago or the "international style" out of Otto Wagner and Peter Behrens in Europe was perforce foreign and inauthentic, except that it was never made clear why in trading one foreign style for another newer one, the same criticism did not apply.

In California at the time, and somewhat later, the architects Maybeck, Howard, Polk, Brown, De Pisis, Mullgardt, and Julia Morgan were quietly active. They did not leave an enormous legacy in quantity or magnificence, but it was an enduring legacy. Contrary to contemporary architectural opinion, they did not create a style in the sense that Chicago did. They responded to the land, the climate, and the materials of the area and created warm, easy residences that modestly began to reduce the hard lines between indoors and outdoors. In their public buildings, however, they continued to work in the classical manner, sometimes with excellent results. Arthur Brown's new city hall *(108–110)*, built to replace the one destroyed in the earthquake, contains one of the most majestic of indoor spaces beneath a rigidly baroque dome. The building is clearly one of the finest public buildings in the United States.

Perhaps it was fortunate that architectural controversy never quite reached the intensity in San Francisco that it did in Chicago until after the quake, for it allowed the city to go about its building free from revolutionary rigor and architectural self-righteousness. Admittedly, the amount of high-rise commercial space necessary was nowhere near that of Chicago and New York, and as a result San Francisco did not attract the number of architects necessary for doctrinaire polemics (some people claim two are all it takes); I suspect, furthermore, that those who did come to San Francisco found arguments about the moral purity of a building irrelevant in that unbelievable and far-removed place.

Although there are more than a handful of fine buildings in San Francisco, contemporary critics and historians are still at a loss in dealing with the west coast. San Francisco never took itself quite so seriously as did the eastern cities, and I think this must have violated a stern moral nerve in both the professional critic and the academic who viewed architecture—all art for that matter—as very serious stuff, and couldn't believe that those westerners, having all that fun in the sun, could produce anything worth discussion.

But that is precisely why we enjoy these buildings. In the frenzy of an explosively growing nation, a city was put together out of buildings that roar with fun, that never (or almost never) take themselves so seriously as to forget how to smile—and they smile well. Nor was their first function forgotten—to house people, and to provide for them an environment that has more to do with life than with the provision of objects for the stimulation of pedantic discussion. Neither did they act as symbols for a reinterpreted democracy, or for giant concentrations of wealth, nor for any of the other liturgies, crotchets, and concerns that the moralistic and the quick-to-indignation need as they chart the purpose of man's work in every artistic flourish. Nothing so deflates or puts out of business the chronicler of art as the unself-conscious, or the work-as-play. The straight-faced novelist, playwright, or poet rooting about looking for the dim meaning of men and women is usually considered a more important craftsman than the comic writer. And black humor is generally considered to have greater moment than just plain humor, the kind that generates well-being rather than wry enlightenment. These houses do not generate wry enlightenment. As a group they were a strange record of architectural style in the latter half of the nineteenth century.

Siegfried Gideon in 1941 published *Space, Time and Architecture*, in which he summed up the prevailing notions of the architectural avant-garde of the twentieth century. "There are whole decades in the second half of the Nineteenth Century in which no architectural work of any significance is encountered. Eclecticism smothered all creative energy." Yes, the houses ran the super-eclectic stylistic gamut of the age—Queen Anne, Victorian Gothic, French Renaissance, Turkish, variegated baroque, German Renaissance, and, mainly, Italianate. True, they were thrown together for the most part without much concern for purity of stylistic grammar, but they had another concern: an attention to those connections between eye and object which suggested that if it feels good, it's moral. And beautiful, too.

The Great Houses

1782 Pacific Avenue.

1911 Sacramento Street.

2019 Pacific Avenue.

2121 Vallejo Street.

623, 627 Baker Street.

1045 Divisadero Street.

1045 Divisadero Street.

201 Buchanan Street.

201 Buchanan Street.

201 Buchanan Street.

3022 Washington Street.

3022 Washington Street.

1550 Page Street.

2004 Gough Street.

1825~1827 Scott Street.

733 Cole Street.

972 Eddy Street.

1911 Sacramento Street.

1544 Page Street.

2002, 2004 Pierce Street.

Riordan's Harbor Branch Saloon. 100, The Embarcadero.

4502 18th Street.

1370~1392 McAllister Street.

263–265 29th Street.

2140 Pierce Street.

1976 California Street.

910 Shotwell Street.

1671, 1673 Golden Gate Avenue.

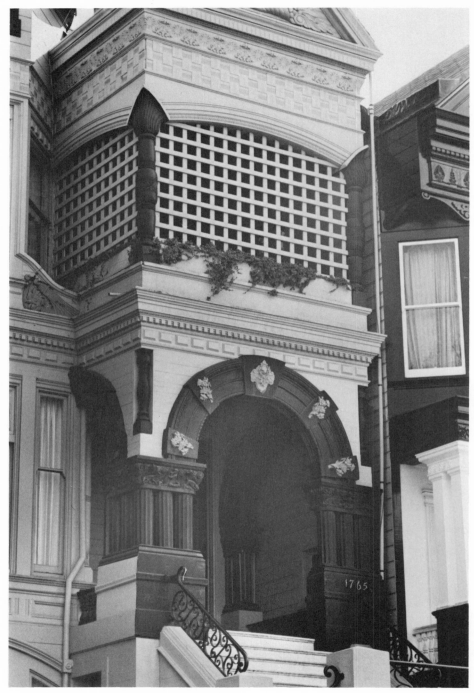

1765 Vallejo Street.

1041 Green Street.

2770, 2772 Sacramento Street.

1705, 1707 Baker Street.

Conservatory, Golden Gate Park. Kennedy Drive.

Conservatory, Golden Gate Park. Kennedy Drive.

Conservatory, Golden Gate Park. Kennedy Drive.

Bardelli's Restaurant. 243 O'Farrell Street. Designed and executed by Otto Dressler.

Walden House. 101 Buena Vista Avenue East.

Women's City Club. Franc Pierce Hammon Memorial Window (1925). Designed by Arthur Mathews. The Oakland Museum.

3497 Sacramento Street.   3497 Sacramento Street.

900 Guerrero Street.

2307 Broadway.

2307 Broadway.

1701 California Street.

1701 California Street.

859 Fulton Street.

461 Oak Street.

928 Divisadero Street.

104 Chattanooga Street.

210 Fair Oaks Street.

2845 Greenwich Street.

2436 Jackson Street.

2735 Clay Street.

2207, 2209 Sutter Street.

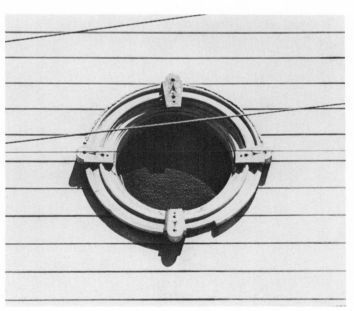

390 Page Street.

3875 20th Street.

4250 23rd Street.

Russian Embassy. 1195–1196 Fulton Street.

"Nobby Clark's Folly," 250 Douglass Street.

"Nobby Clark's Folly. " 250 Douglass Street.

759, 761 Oak Street.

1919 Sacramento Street.

2910 Bush Street.

1900 Webster Street.

770 Ashbury Street.

3404 Clay Street.

1716~1722 Baker Street.

2620 Laguna Street.

2110~2116 Divisadero Street.

2110 Divisadero Street.

City Hall. Civic Center, Van Ness Avenue.

City Hall. Civic Center, Van Ness Avenue.

City Hall. Civic Center, Van Ness Avenue.

City Hall. Civic Center, Van Ness Avenue.

City Hall. Civic Center, Van Ness Avenue.

City Hall. Civic Center, Van Ness Avenue.

R. Matteucci & Co., 229 Columbus Avenue.

Sheet Metal Workers Hall, 244 Guerrero Street.

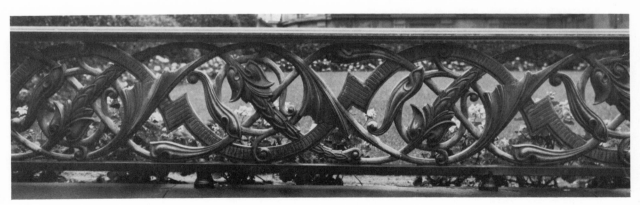

James J. Flood Mansion, bronze fence, 500 block, California Street.

802 Page Street.

2901 Mission Street.

210 Frederick Street.

3021 Washington Street.

2773 Clay Street.

229 Jersey Street.

1347 McAllister Street.

1347 McAllister Street.

Bank of America. 1 Powell Street.

Columbus Tower, with Transamerica Pyramid (left), and Chinese Cultural Center (right). 141 Columbus Avenue.

1818 Green Street.

2000 Baker Street.

1–7 Buena Vista Avenue, East.

600 block, Buchanan Street.

1834 California Street.

2665 Laguna Street.

1901 Scott Street.

1016 Pierce Street.

2007 Franklin Street.

2007 Franklin Street.

2007 Franklin Street.

999 Fell Street.

Old San Francisco Opera House, 4700 Newcomb Street.

Old San Francisco Opera House, 4700 Newcomb Street.

70 Liberty Street.

773 Turk Street.

773 Turk Street.

773 Turk Street.

1067 Green Street.

2645 Gough Street.

Levi Strauss Factory.   200 block, Valencia Street.

Levi Strauss Factory.   200 block, Valencia Street.

Levi Strauss Factory.   200 block, Valencia Street.

3816 22nd Street.

3501 Clay Street.

171~183 Collingwood Street.

1919–1933 Greenwich Street.

309, 311 Steiner Street.

309 Steiner Street.

400~412 Central Avenue.

294 Page Street.

294 Page Street.

294 Page Street.

2411 Webster Street.

2411 Webster Street.

2006~2012 Pierce Street.

722 Waller Street.

575 Liberty Street.

401 Baker Street.

2710, 2712 California Street.

2026 California Street.

2026 California Street.

2026 California Street.

708 Montgomery Street.

1454 Valencia Street.

—(165)—

545 Sanchez Street.

1745–1753 Pine Street.

2057 Bush Street.

2733, 2735 California Street.

The Vedanta Society Temple. 2961–2963 Webster Street.

The Vedanta Society Temple. 2961–2963 Webster Street.

The Vedanta Society Temple. 2961~2963 Webster Street.

The Vedanta Society Temple. 2961–2963 Webster Street.

2022~2018 California Street.

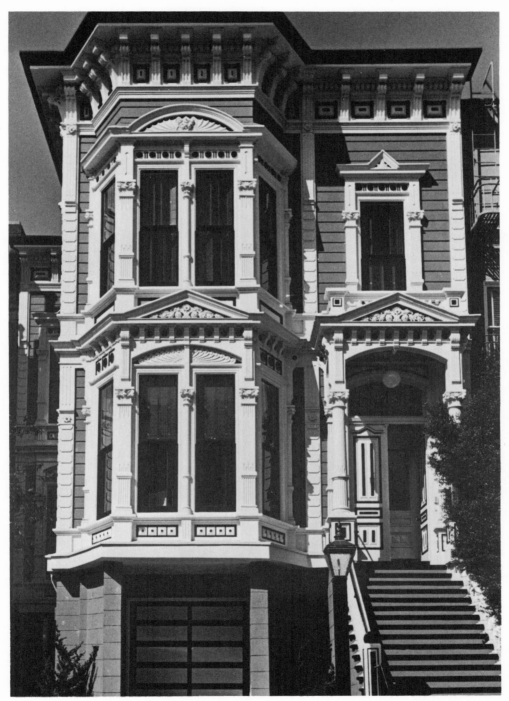

2018 California Street.

888–896 14th Street.

251 Laguna Street.

1326–1330 Masonic Avenue.

1326 Masonic Avenue.

Hobart Building (foreground), with Wells Fargo Bank Main Office (rear).   582 Market Street.

—(180)—

Phelan Building. 760 Market Street.

2667 Sacramento Street.

3100 Clay Street.

2180 Filbert Street.

116–120 Divisadero Street.

451 Fair Oaks Street.

1812, 1814 Pacific Avenue.

68 Fair Oaks Street.

2527, 2531 Washington Street.

Epilogue

uite early in the latter half of the twentieth century, the mechanisms born of social pressure, human need for change, and developmental greed reduced block upon block of San Francisco houses to the few sad and fewer grand remaining residences, remnants of that prouder time in San Francisco from the 1850s to the quake. Especially out in the Western Addition, they were destroyed. Of those that remain, some are still painted and tended to; others stand vacant, hollow, underused, gutted by neglect, fire, rising taxes, and the misfortune of being located in what has been designated a redevelopment area. The façades are now peeling victims of a social scrofula, their windows blind eyes staring out on a time that thought it could pass them by, reminders of the life that birthed them and the social changes that nourished them from simple box to bizarre exclamation. Lonely brooding relics, they wait by the edge of arteries once busy with horse and wagon but now crazy with cars, wait for their turn to feel the blow of the wrecker's ball. In the late 1950s and early 1960s, acres of that intricate real estate succumbed to the destruction that is inevitable when the social and financial arrangements necessary to deal gently with change are lacking. San Francisco has not been alone among American cities to employ those surgical flourishes that make whole areas of the city the refuge of the poor, the non-white, the foreign, and those who, stubborn beyond evidence of reality, chose to inhabit and tend (however meagerly) to those places where the intricacy of civilized city living was matched by the intricacy of the surround.

If asked to simplify, I would say that the death of vast areas of small, medium, and large cities was caused by the mechanisms of the Federal Housing Administration and the National Highway Act and its concomitant network of highways and superhighways built during the 1950s and 1960s. The housing shortage was acute at the end of World War II, and the mass of housing built, necessary to fill the gap, responded to a dream of Americans—each man in his castle surrounded by a plot of land over which he holds absolute dominion if not title. The dream was the residue of an agrarian nation—a nation which, in spite of a rhetoric of unity, had no shared culture, no shared root language or customs, a nation of ghettos which, as economic freedom allowed, permitted the ghettos to grow smaller and smaller until, in the suburbs, the unit of the ghetto was one family living the faded fantasy of the agrarian dream.

In truth it could be said that America has always hated its cities as well as the city's inhabitants. Smart money, city slickers, fast women: all collided in popular rural white Protestant consciousness. The city had always been a port of entry and a holding ground for strangers—until accents were lost, cuisines altered, and life styles blurred, and the strangers too assimilated the desire and fled into the agrarian dream. The Highway Act merely provided the legal and financial mechanisms that made possible the roads by which access was gained to hitherto closed areas of countryside, making it possible to live the rural fantasy in what was viewed as country and still work where the commerce was, in the city. It is also to the point that both the Highway Act and the F.H.A. provided an incredible number of jobs as well as economic fluidity for most. Fluidity that made it possible to buy the cars that others built,

1860 Turk Street.

101 Pierce Street.

to drive them on the roads that others built, to go to houses that others built, after working in the city that others had to pay for, leaving whole areas of the city to corrode through neglect. The remaining inhabitants—the old, the poor, the black, the immigrants (and the stubborn)—usually stayed behind not from choice but because they lacked the means to join the flight to the suburbs. In San Francisco, they came to occupy the houses out in the Western Addition that were deserted by the affluent and not-so-affluent whites.

As a result of shifting focus, financial and real estate interest, and crafty naïveté, the Western Addition became a testing ground for yet another set of arrangements that was to solve the "problem" that had been caused by previous arrangements. The Western Addition was found to be a slum and the solution to that problem was thought to be redevelopment; the wholesale clearance of these houses, houses that housed the problem, began. Forget that the problem was people; what was important was that the problem be removed,

1153 Oak Street.

1153 Oak Street.

1800 block, Sutter Street.

fecting the rehabilitation of hundreds of other pre-quake houses and certain old public buildings throughout the city. As a program of building new firehouses was undertaken, the city offered at auction a number of older ones which, after purchase, were remade into professional office buildings and private homes. Lovingly altered on the inside, the exteriors remained as they were; even the towers were retained, large vertical volumes on which the lengths of hoses were once hauled by block and tackle to hang and dry after each use (60-1). The old Opera House (134-5), used for a time by the great Belasco, was rescued from decay by the city itself even though permanent specific use for it has not yet been found. Out in the Mission District, the Levi Strauss Company refused to bow before the rules of strict industrial efficiency and chose to remain in its original factory (142-3), saving hundreds of local jobs as well as its marvelous building, while providing playground space in the parking lot for local youths on weekends.

For the most part, we don't know who built and designed these buildings, or if indeed anybody did design them as we know the term today, since the records went up in flames when the old city hall burned in the 1906 fire and quake. But it is not in these origins that their value exists but in their presence, and it is that presence that must be preserved.

Do we need to ask why we should take special care to save these wooden beauties—and grotesqueries—to make available or to invent the economic means necessary to spare them? Immediate change is not only incomprehensible without reference to what came before, but the direction of that change becomes totally unpredictable. Derelict ruins and patched artifacts of previous

and as a result hundreds of these buildings were destroyed. Many of the houses had deteriorated beyond redemption through neglect, but others, many of them among the best, went before the bite of the bulldozer, leaving their displaced residents on their own to find alternate housing. And many continue to fall, chewed to bits and ground to trash by engines of greed, indifference, and a seeming inability to deal with a measure of mess as well as age.

And yet, while this ruthless clearance of many blocks was going on, individual concern was af-

1800 block, Sutter Street.

times serve much the same function as picture albums, museums, and athletic records; they remind us where we have been.

There is at root, however, a much simpler and more direct reason why a strong effort should be made to save, if not all, at least enough of the very best of these buildings so that they remain a vital and active piece of the city and not museum pieces: They will never happen again. All of the overt and direct, subtle and even mysterious sets of interrelationships, pressures, and people that gave birth to these houses will never come together at the same time and place again — ever. As such, they are unique, but beyond being unique they are wonderful, and if they go, San Francisco may be newer, neater, and, heaven help us, even in better taste, some might argue; but it will also be a city in which an amputation of extremity has taken place, for we would be cutting off the start, the base line against which San Francisco measures itself. It is in the intimacies enjoyed by the eye as the light plays over the scrollwork of these buildings that the city exists architecturally, in fact exists at all.

1800 block, Sutter Street.

1800 block, Sutter Street.

1800 block, Sutter Street.

Street Address Index

Index of Buildings

From the Authors

The painter Kandinski said that "Art is the child of the times and the mother of our emotions." Yet the art of the past, whether a Victorian mansion or a pre-Columbian idol, rarely intrudes into the plastic melange of our visual world, except on special occasions.

While every building is an event of a particular epoch, frozen in time, photography's most outstanding quality seems to be the ability to preserve whatever instant or event toward which it is directed. And often, all that may remain of a fine architectural work is an empty lot and a photograph.

We can only see as much in any work of art as we bring to it; the business of seeing is a growth process that should never end, and which can awaken our undeveloped sense of time and the past.

—Curt Bruce

The Great Houses of San Francisco is an attempt at placing these buildings within the context of their time in a breezy anecdotal manner that perhaps conveys some of the reasons why they happened.

The book attempts to demonstrate that what happened, happened because of some very local and private circumstances—a web of circumstances particular to San Francisco as one outpost of the "Victorian Age," sharing tendencies (the generosity of scale, virtue of civic pride, a persuasive and broad sensuousness), but also generating and displaying individual solutions to larger problems. A lot of what went down there was the result of San Francisco going from a raunchy outpost, tucked in the fold of some treeless rolling hills forming the end of a peninsula, to a cosmopolitan city in less than forty years, a telescoped example of urban growth. The direction it took was due to the kinds of fortune hunters and misfits who found their way to San Francisco and California, and to the kind of fortunes that were made.

These houses read now as a graph of the rising fortunes of the city and its inhabitants. What few first structures remain are small and void of decoration—simple boxes with pitched or slightly sloping roofs. Silver and gold, railroads, and an exploitive trade with China caused San Francisco to become, by the 1890s an extremely tasty place to seek and make one's fortune, and the façades of the city reflected this affluence. Block upon block of homes were built out in the Western

Addition to house the growing population. These tract houses of the late-nineteenth century, designed and built by carpenters for the most part, are the confident beauties we admire. As intricate and chased as a fine rifle stock of the day, they shared in the Victorian passion both here and in England to decorate, to enrich their physical surrounds, and by doing so, to enrich themselves.

—Thomas Aidala